Made in the USA
Middletown, DE
05 March 2023

26225208R00064